WELCOME HOME, MUFFIN!

Written By:

ELINOR SITRISH

Welcome Home, Muffin!

May you always see the world through the eyes of a child

Dedicated to:

My beloved husband and family near and far,

Thank you for your endless love and support!

My precious Lady & Charlie,

Thank you for your unconditional love.

Forever in my heart,

Elinor.

It's Sunday! ... and it's flea market time!

The Hope family is out the door bright and early with Adam leading the way.

They love going to the nearby flea market every Sunday.

There's so much going on! Like the smell and taste of freshly cooked food, fun music and beautiful art.

Adam loves all of the booths at the market but his favorite has grilled corn and fresh lemonade juice!

Mmmmm Yummy!

Oh Sunday, what a fun day!

Adam loves going up and down the aisles and tables full of unique and wonderful things.

Next to one of the booths is one that Adam never seen before.

Dog Rescue? There is just a man, a table and lots of papers. I wonder what they selling here?

Underneath the table Adam notices a few cardboard boxes and tiny little noses poking out.

"OOOO, Puppies!!!"

They are all so small, so fluffy and soooo cute!

"Mom, Dad...look!" Adam screamed from excitement.

"Please, oh, please...can I get a puppy?"

"Well Adam, a puppy is not a toy you know... You have to take care of it all the time.

You need to feed it, train, bathe and clean it!"

"Mom is right," said Dad, "a puppy needs to be taken care of and requires a lot of attention and care.

It's just not the right time to get you a puppy. Perhaps, next year"

But I want a puppy so badly, Adam thinks to himself. He lets out a deep, long sigh "Ahhhh, okay I guess I'll just have to wait until next year".

Adam turns his head to look at the puppies one last time.

The man at the booth picks-up one of the puppies and puts him in a separate box.

Curious as he is, Adam turns to the nice man who seemed to be in-charge of the booth.

"Sir, why is this dog for free? And why does he look so sad and scared?"

As he adds more puppies to the box, the man explains; "Well, this, is a rescued dog and his name is Muffin.

You can call me Tom, by the way".

"Hello Mr. Tom, I'm Adam.
What's a rescued dog?"

"A rescue" says Tom, "are dogs that we save from a bad environment and try to find them a good home.

We rescued Muffin because he was not taken care of. That's why he is so sad".

Adam moves closer to the box, "Hello Muffin. My name is Adam."

Slowly offering his hand hoping that Muffin would maybe sniff or wag his tail like most dogs.

Instead, Muffin whimpered and lowered his head.

"It's alright Muffin", says Adam, "don't be scared."

"I think you are a very nice and brave dog and I just want to be your friend.

I promise I won't hurt you."

"Adam, it's time to go home now."

"Okay, Dad. I'm coming!"

"Goodbye Mr. Tom. Goodbye Muffin.
I promise I'll come visit you again next week."

A week went by and its Sunday again. As usual, the Hope family is on the way to the flea market.

Adam is especially excited to see Muffin!

He skips the usual booths including the lemonade stand and runs straight to see the puppies.

"Hey there, buddy!"
Adam said, cheerfully greeting Muffin.

"It's good to see you again!
See, I'm back as I promised..."

Adam reached out to
Muffin hoping to be cheerful this time.

But Muffin was still sad.
He just lowered his big brown eyes.

The visit flew by even quicker this time.

"So long little buddy. See you next week!"

Adam kept looking back at his new pal just wishing he would wag his tail.

"It's okay son, I guess Muffin just doesn't trust people yet. We'll try again next week" said Dad.

And once again, the long week passed by slowly, but now it's Sunday again.

Adam is all washed-up, dressed and ready to go.

As usual, he headed straight for Tom's booth looking forward to seeing Muffin once more.

But...wait! What?!? It can't be!!!

Muffin's box was empty!

OH NO!!!

"Mr. Tom...Mr. Tom! Where is Muffin??"
Adam asked with tears in his eyes and his heart
sinking to the ground.

"Oh, I'm sorry Adam. Someone came and took him
already. But if it makes you feel better, he is now
with a really nice family and I know

he will be looked after." said
Tom trying to make Adam feel better.

"But...but, he was my friend!
I promised him I'll come back!
And I didn't get the chance to see him one last time!"
Adam said, sobbing.

"Don't be sad Adam" said his Dad.

"You should be happy that your little buddy has finally found a new home and that from now on he is going to have a happier and better life."

Adam pulled his shoulders up and wiped his tears.

"I guess you are right, Dad.
You know, I'm going to miss him a lot!
I will never forget him."

"And I'm sure he will never forget you.
Now lets get you your favorite corn and lemonade!

what do you say?"

The corn and lemonade didn't taste as good today...

Adam is sad the whole way home and goes straight to his room.

But wait...

What is this? There is a box on my bed...
A present? ...for me?? "What is it Mom?"

"Well...I guess you'll have to open it if you want to find out"

"Yes Adam, come on, open it!" said Dad.

I wonder what it can be. Is it a toy?
what kind of a toy?

Thinking that nothing would cheer him up today
as Adam removes the bow off the box.

Adam was wrong because this present made him
jump from excitement!

Guess what's in the box???

"It's Muffin!!! Oh, Muffin, I missed you so muchhh!"

This time Muffin was wagging his tail and licking
Adam's face!

"Ahhh! Mom! Dad! Did you see that?
He licked my face."

"That means he is happy now Adam".

"Oh! I love you so much. I promise I'll take good
care of you. You will never be sad again."

"Oh gosh, what's that smell?" said Mom.

"Ewwww!" said Adam covering his little nose,

"I think Muffin just...farted!"

They all looked at each other and burst out laughing, as Muffin wagged his tail.

"Welcome home, Muffin!" said Adam.

"Welcome home, Muffin!" Said Mr. and Mrs. Hope

From that day on, Muffin became a part of a family and received lots and lots of love.